GROW UP AND LOVE YOUR BODY!

The Complete Girls' Guide to Growing Up Age 8-12 incl. Body-Care and Self-Esteem Special

Sarah P. Weston

ISBN - 9798831701241

CONTENTS

INTRODUCTION

Being a young girl, you may be experiencing many changes in the way you look, the way you feel and things in your life. At the age of eight, you are still in primary school and you might have interests like spending time with your school friends at home or playing with your favourite toys.

The next few years will be a transition. By the time you reach the age of twelve, you are in high school and you might have started going through a process that is called puberty. This is one of the biggest changes that you will ever go through in your life. Typically, it starts around the age of ten or eleven but it can start even earlier or later. It will usually last for most of your teenage years, taking you into womanhood.

With all of these changes happening around you, it can feel like a lot of pressure on your young shoulders. Therefore, it is important to be aware of what the changes are so that you understand what is happening to your body and your feelings as you grow up. By being more aware of what is happening, you can learn ways to deal with the changes without getting upset, confused or stressed about them.

There is a lot of pressure on young girls in the media, television, movies and celebrity culture to look good. So, you might feel that you do not live up to the way society thinks that you should look. We will look at different ways to learn to understand how your body and mind work and explore different things that can help you to learn to love your body and appreciate yourself.

In this book, we will explore the different ways your body and your mind are changing right now and how to cope with those changes. Most importantly, we will focus on how to learn to love your body and how to make healthy changes if you need to make them.

Your self-esteem comes from who you are on the inside and is something that no one can take away from you. Whether you are very smart, a talented athlete or a kind and generous person, everyone has skills and it is important that you are aware of your good qualities so that you can have confidence in yourself and learn to appreciate all the good things about yourself.

WHY ARE BODY IMAGE AND SELF-ESTEEM IMPORTANT?

Throughout your childhood, you might not have been conscious of the way you look. Some girls are worried about their looks from a very young age but for others, this tends to happen as they approach double-figures.

From the age of eight onwards, you will notice that there are some changes to your body as you begin to mature and it can be really important for your confidence to have a good, healthy body image that you will maintain for the rest of your life.

For a large part of human history, there has been a big focus on the way that girls and women look. If you have ever been to a museum or art gallery, you might have seen some old paintings and portraits of women that show what those artists thought female beauty was. Of course, the idea of what it means to be beautiful has changed over the years but as a girl, you will notice that some people focus on your looks.

Low self-esteem means that you might feel sad and stressed in some way. The important thing is to remember that self-esteem starts on side and that you're wonderfully unique and truly special.

Sometimes, it is easy to lose your self-esteem. People can be mean and sometimes they can make comments that make you feel really bad about yourself. If that has happened to you, then there are some ways to feel better.

○ If you are clean, dressed in a way that makes you feel comfortable and you eat well, you are doing amazing!

○ Focus on how amazing your body really is: every cell in your body is alive and each one works with all the others to create amazing things every day.

○ Cut yourself some slack: if you are too hard on yourself because you are feeling bad, you will actually feel even worse. Spend some time looking at your good qualities and take care of yourself.

○ Be around positive people: you don't want to spend time around people who make negative comments to you because that will only make you feel worse. If you have a relative or family friend who you have to be around, talk to someone and try to avoid the person who makes you feel bad as much as you possibly can.

PUBERTY AND YOUR BODY CHANGES

Puberty is a big life event for every girl and it is something that everyone, both girls and boys, goes through. All your life, from when you were a little baby and toddler, you have probably grown used to your body changing slightly but not significantly. Puberty is the time when you change from being a little girl to maturing into a woman. It doesn't happen overnight and it will last for most of your teens.

As you approach puberty and start to go through it, your body will make a lot of changes. You can start puberty as young as the age of eight and as late as the age of fourteen. While there are a few girls who begin puberty earlier or later than these ages, that is rarer.

The first sign of puberty that you will start to notice is that your breasts will start to develop. At first, you might feel that your chest is very tender. For some girls, one breast starts to develop before the other. This is very normal and it is nothing to worry about. Of course, you might feel selfconscious if one breast starts to grow while the other one remains flat but you can feel reassured that the second one will catch up very quickly.

Another early sign that you have begun to go through puberty is that you will start to grow hair between your legs and you might also see that more hair grows on your arms and legs. Again, some girls feel self-conscious about this new hair, especially when you are going swimming at school or changing in front of other people before and after your physical education and gym classes in the locker rooms. However, every girl goes through the same thing and nobody will judge you for it. Your friends and peers are probably experiencing something very similar right now too.

It can be helpful to talk to your friends about the changes that you are experiencing in your body because this is a good way to find support from other people who understand as they are also going through it. If you have a close supportive friend or group of friends, you can ease your worries by talking to them as you will realise that you are normal in going through these changes.

As puberty continues, you will start to notice even more changes, especially after the first year. Your breasts will keep growing and they will seem rounder and fuller than they used to be. The hair on your pubic area will also become thicker and curly. You will get more hair in other places too, such as under your arm and even on your upper lip. You might have friends who shave this hair or go with their parents to a beauty salon to have it removed. This is a personal choice for every girl and it is important to do what feels right for you. If it is upsetting you, really making you feel bad or worried and you want to shave the hair, then there is nothing wrong with doing that. But, do not feel like there is pressure to shave if you do not want to.

At this point in puberty, you will also find that you sweat more than you used to. You might find that your forehead and face become sweatier when it is hot or when you exercise. Your armpits might also sweat more. Sometimes, this can lead to body odour. So, it is important to choose a safe and natural antiperspirant or deodorant. It is a good idea to talk to an older female relative or family friend, like your mum or an aunt, who can recommend some good brands of deodorant for you to use. They can also help to show you how to apply it so that you do not put too much on or get it all over your clothes, as that can leave white marks on the material.

Acne is a big part of puberty that affects most girls but it can be more or less severe from one girl to another. If you notice that you have spots like blackheads or whiteheads, it is a great idea to ask your parents or guardians to buy you a really good cleanser. Having acne, especially when it is severe can really affect your self-confidence and this is totally normal. Acne normally goes away when you get older. If it is *really* bad, you might want to talk to your parents about taking you to a doctor. There are some special treatments that can help you.

Getting taller and gaining some body weight are two other effects of puberty. During the first four or five years of puberty, you can grow between 5 cm and 7.5 cm every year until you reach the height that you are going to be as an adult. This can be a big change for you to deal with and you will notice that you have to buy lots of new clothes to wear as your body changes so much.

Remember that all of these changes are **positive**. While change can be really scary, it is important to understand exactly what is happening to you. You are starting on a fantastic journey into the future, leaving behind your childhood and heading toward becoming a woman. It can be a long journey and there might be times when you will feel sad or worried along the way but it can be a beautiful time when you turn from a duckling into a swan.

CHANGING FEELINGS AND SELF-CONFIDENCE

Puberty can change your body a lot but it can also change your feelings and emotions too. When you start puberty, your body begins to produce substances that are called hormones. In girls, the two main hormones that your body will make are oestrogen and progesterone.

These two hormones are the things that cause some of the changes in your body but they might also make your mood start to change too. During your childhood, you might have noticed that when you felt happy, you kept feeling happy for a long time unless something bad happened to make you feel sad or worried.

As you go through puberty and you have more of these hormones in your body, your mood will change more quickly. You might feel happy for a while and then suddenly feel sad or angry for no reason. Sometimes, this can be very scary because it can feel like you do not have control over your emotions.

Just like with the changes to your body, the changes to your mind and your feeling are experienced by everyone at your age. It can last through your teen years before the hormones finally start to settle down and your body and brain become used to them.

However, although you know that these mood swings do not last forever, it can be difficult for you to experience them right now and it can make you feel annoyed and frustrated. It can also make you lose some confidence because it is hard for you to be out of control with your feelings. The good news is that there are some ways that you can help yourself to cope and boost your self-confidence in the process:

⭕ **Talk to someone:** Talking to a parent, friend or teacher is a great way to share your feelings and know that you are not alone in the way that you feel. You can get advice from older people who once went through it themselves or get support from friends your own age and share the current experiences that you are going through.

○ Realise that you are not the only one going through this: Sometimes, it can be important to remind yourself that other people are going through the same thing. Both girls and boys experience changes in their moods during this stage in their life. So, when you are feeling frustrated or struggling, remember that you are not alone.

○ **Distract yourself with a hobby:** This can be a good time to find a creative hobby to distract yourself from the waves of thoughts that are affecting you. You can take up activities like painting, drawing, writing, singing or playing a musical instrument. You can even join a sports team or club.

○ **Try breathing exercises:** When it feels like your moods are out of control, you can breathe in and hold your breath for a few seconds, counting to ten while you do this. If you repeat this a few times, you might notice that it calms you and makes you feel better and less stressed than you felt before.

O **Don't slack on your sleep:** Make sure that you are getting enough sleep every night. Your body is growing and changing and lots of new things are happening in your brain. Even if you are feeling worried or stressed, it is important to get enough rest as feeling tired can also make you more likely to feel upset.

O **Don't be afraid to let your emotions show:** If there are times when you want to laugh like crazy or just have a cry, it is better to let yourself do this instead of holding it all inside. You can actually make yourself feel better just by letting out the emotions.

Tell yourself that you are worthy: During this time, if your self-confidence takes a tip, remind yourself of all the good things that you have to offer. This is a time when you are blossoming and that is a beautiful thing. Remember that and it will help you through the harder times.

FRIENDSHIPS

At this time in your life, you will notice that you might experience a lot of changes in your friendships. Some of your friends might drift away, especially when you leave primary school and go to high school as that is a time of big change. Your old friends might want to have new experiences and they are going through changes in their feelings too.

It can be difficult to lose old friends but you should keep in mind that even if your old friends find new friendship groups, you can do the same thing too! Of course, if you do not have good self-confidence, then it can be more difficult to make new friends as you might be shy around new people. As you work on boosting your confidence and self-esteem, you are likely to find that it becomes easier to reach out to new people.

Even when you are always with the same group of friends, they can sometimes still affect you in ways that you might not expect. Body image can be affected by friends.

It is important to remember that every girl is different. The way we look is partly because we have something called genes in us. We get these genes from our parents and it is like a recipe to decide how we look. We cannot change these genes as they are fixed before we are even born.

As you grow up, loving your body is really important and sometimes, your friendships and school experiences can be a big part of this.

There have been many girls that have felt upset when one of their classmates says that they are "prettier" than they are. Or, if a boy you like asks out another girl in your class, this can also make you feel sad. You might wonder if there is something wrong with you or if you do not look good enough for that boy to like you.

Here is a secret: *different people have different ideas about what makes someone beautiful.*

You might see that one boy in your class is interested in a blonde-haired, blue-eyed girl. Another boy in your class might like a girl with dark hair and brown eyes. No matter what your skin colour, hair colour, height, weight, shape or size, there are people out there who will see you as beautiful. You might have a friend or classmate who you think is really pretty. Even if you think that you have flaws or blemishes, you probably have friends and schoolmates who are jealous of the way that you look!

HOW TO REACT TO BULLIES

Bullying is a horrible experience that happens to a lot of girls. It can happen in many ways like at school or on the internet. It can even happen from a sibling or family member. Adults can also bully children too and this can be even more difficult because it can seem like they are bigger and stronger than you.

There are lots of reasons why bullies might pick on someone and if you are being bullied about the way you look, it can be hard to grow up to love your body. If your bully tells you that you are ugly, fat, skinny or that you have horrible hair or teeth, it can deeply affect you.

When you are being bullied, it can make you feel very sad. You might not want to talk to other people and you might just feel like hiding away in your room where nobody can see you. It can even be tempting to give in and lose or gain weight depending on what the bully tells you is "wrong" with you. Your emotions might feel constantly confused and you may often ask: "Why me? What did I do wrong? What did I do to deserve this?"

The truth is bullying is not caused by the victim (you). It is always the fault of the bully. Of course, knowing this doesn't always help you feel better when someone is picking on you and making you feel bad about yourself.

So, what are the best ways to tackle bullies?

1. **Walk away** – Whether the bullying is happening at school or online, try not to get into a conversation with the bully. If they come over to you and start to talk to you, do not even answer them. If they send you a message online or on your phone, delete it without reading it.

2. **Find a friend to spend time with** – There really is safety in numbers. If you have a good friend or friendship group at school, try and be with them as often as possible. The bully is less likely to target you when there are a lot of other people around, supporting you.

3. **Do not give in to the anger** – It can be easy to want to shout and scream at the bully when they say mean things to you but then you are showing them that they have upset you and this is what they want. Showing them that you do not care about what they say is not the reaction they expect.

4. **Talk to a parent or teacher** – If the bullying gets worse and it is really affecting you or they threaten you physically, it is important to report them. It can be hard and you might think that telling someone will make it even worse but the truth is that the bully will probably not stop until an adult steps in to help make them stop it.

5. **Spend time rebuilding your confidence** – Bullying can often take away a lot of your self-confidence. It can make you feel small, worthless and ugly. It can take some work to make yourself feel better again. Often, it just takes time to allow yourself to heal from the bullying but if you notice that you do not seem to be recovering or getting better, you might need to talk to a counsellor or therapist. Talk to your parents and be honest with them

about how you are feeling and they will be able to decide with you what is the best thing to do.

Many girls – and boys too – experiencing bullying in their lives. Even adults can be bullied sometimes so you are not alone if you have been bullied. It can take some time to recover from it and feel better about yourself and what has happened. Make sure that you have people around you to support you and do not be afraid to talk about how it has made you feel because that is the best way to start to feel better.

DIET AND EXERCISE

Eating healthily and finding a form of exercise you enjoy are two great ways to have fun. You'll have lots of energy and you can build self-esteem from within.

You need substances called vitamins, minerals, protein, fat and carbohydrates for your body to work well. Getting a healthy balance will also help you to enjoy yourself more.

Becoming more aware of the way you look is natural, particularly as you enter puberty. There is a lot of pressure on girls to look a certain way, but try happiness comes from how you are on the inside. You are unique and that's plenty to be proud of — there is only one you!

To show you how everyone is different, and that being different is okay, we're going to answer so common questions.

How important is a healthy diet?

Eating at healthy diet will give you energy to have fun and try new things. You can be outside playing, inside reading, or just dreaming about what you want to do when you're all grown up.

Can you have a healthy diet and still have a treat?

Of course! Everyone loves a sweet treat from time to time and there's nothing wrong with treating yourself.

Do you have to exercise to be feel good about yourself?

Exercise is a great way to feel happy, but different people enjoy it in different ways. Ignore the pressure of others and look for a way to stay active that you enjoy. If you're doing something that's not fun, look for something that will put a smile back on your face.

Here's a few things you might want to try to see if you like them...

Exercise ideas:

○ **Walking:** This is a really easy way to get some exercise into your day every single day. You can ask a friend, parent or sibling to go for a walk with you after school so that you do not just sit down in front of the television. If you have a dog, it can also be good to take your dog for a walk and it can be really fun too.

○ **Running:** Running is a very popular form of exercise and you can just run on the pavement or you can join a team at your school. If you really like it, you can even join a running club. For people who take running seriously, there are lots of different events and distances. Some people are better at sprinting (short distances like 100m or 200m). Sprinters tend to be faster but they cannot run as far as long-distance runners. Long-distance running can range between running distances like 1500 m and marathon running (just over 26 miles). Some girls start running for fun and someday they find themselves at the Olympic Games and even win a medal.

O **Gymnastics**: A sport that is very beautiful to perform and watch, gymnastics can not only help you to get in shape but can make you feel really good and graceful. It can help you to be more flexible and build your muscle tone. The American gymnast, Dominique Moceanu, won a gold medal in gymnastics at the Olympic Games at the age of only 14 in 1996.

O **Tennis:** This is a great sport where you can use speed, skill and cleverness to win games. One of the best things about tennis for a young girl is that if you are good at it and you ever decide to do this sport as a job, you will earn equal prize money to the men.

O **Football:** Girls' football has become more popular in the past few years and there are lots of girls' teams all over the country now. It is not only good for helping you to stay fit but it is a good way to make friends and learn to work as a part of a team. As you get older, you can make friendships with teammates that can last for a lifetime.

○ **Swimming:** If you enjoy the water, swimming is a good choice for exercise. Swimming is considered a "low impact" activity which means that it does not put a strain on your muscles and joints in the same way as activities like running can do. So, if you have any reason that you need to be careful when it comes to exercising, swimming can really help you.

No matter which one you try, the most important thing is to find a form of exercise that you feel comfortable with and enjoy. There's no pressure at this age, or any age for that matter, to fit into a strict category. You're unique, you're special, and we think you're wonderful. There's definitely going to be a great way to stay active out there that will make you smile before you know it.

GOOD HYGIENE

As you approach puberty or start to go through it, you might notice that you have more body odours than you used to. However, there are many kinds of good hygiene that you can practise so that your body feels clean and you feel confident. If you do not have good hygiene, you can get skin infections, have decaying teeth and smell bad.

Now is the best time to get into a good hygiene routine that you can continue for the rest of your life. Here are some of the top tips for making sure that you look, feel and smell squeaky clean every single day:

O **Brush your teeth:** This might sound obvious but brushing your teeth can be more than just using a toothbrush against your teeth for 20 seconds every morning. You should try to brush your teeth at least two to three times every day. It is also a good idea to use dental floss too, especially at night before you go to bed. Mouthwash can make your breath smell fresh too. There are several different brands of special kids' mouthwashes and you can even get unbranded versions that are cheaper. By taking care of your teeth, you can stop them from decaying or even falling out one day. You will also boost your confidence because you will know that your breath smells fresh.

O **Take baths or showers every day:** Bathing and showering daily are very important, especially when you start to go through puberty or start your period. This can wash away the germs that collect on your body and stop you from smelling bad. It can also make your hair look nice and clean and shiny and prevent it from looking greasy or stringy.

O **Change your clothes regularly:** Germs can collect on clothes when you have worn them. Germs from your own body and also from the environment outside can stay on your clothes. If you want to feel confident in the way that you look, putting on fresh clothes every morning is a good idea for looking and smelling good.

O **Change your sanitary pads and tampons:** When sanitary pads and tampons are not changed regularly, they can start to smell. If tampons are not changed every so often, this can also lead to serious health risks like Toxic Shock Syndrome. So, it is very important to keep period hygiene in mind.

O **Shaving your legs and armpits:** Puberty brings body hair and as you grow more, you might notice that some of your friends choose to shave their legs and underarms. This is entirely your choice and you should not feel like you are under pressure to shave if you do not want to. The benefit of shaving your underarms can be that you will reduce any odour from sweating, such as during gym class at school. However, you should talk to your mum and dad about whether it is the right choice for you.

COPING WITH PERIODS

One of the biggest changes that you will experience at this point in your life is the start of your periods. Periods happen to every girl and woman for many years of their lives. They tend to start around the age of twelve but they can begin earlier or later than this.

Often, girls can get their periods anytime between the ages of 10 years old and 15 years old. By the time you reach your mid-teens, you will almost certainly have started your period, if you have not already started them now.

There can be some signs that you are going to start your period very soon. These signs are similar to the ones that you experience when you first start going through puberty. If your breasts might have started to develop or if they have felt tender, this can mean that you have already started developing and moving toward a point where your body is ready to start having a period. Also, if you have hair under your arms and between your legs, this can be another sign that your period is coming soon.

When you first get your period, it can be very scary. Your body is doing something new for the first time and it might be confusing and hard to understand why this is happening to you. Of course, finding blood between your legs would be a scary experience for anyone but learning about periods and understanding what they are and why they happen can make it a lot easier for you to deal with.

Periods start because your body is changing. As we talked about in an earlier chapter, when you reach puberty, your body starts to produce hormones. These hormones are chemicals that send messages from one part of your body to another and tell different parts of your body what to do.

The hormones in your body mean that the lining of your womb, which is sometimes called a uterus, starts to thicken. This happens because your body is going to release an egg from your ovaries. The womb is prepared for the release of the egg. For older women who are ready to be sexually active, they can make a baby when a man's sperm attaches to the egg. However, when you are not going to make a baby, the thickened lining of the womb is not needed and it breaks down.

The broken-down lining of the womb is released and this is why you bleed because your body is getting rid of the unneeded tissue. Every month, the same process happens in a cycle so you will most likely bleed monthly. However, many girls will notice that when they first get their periods, they do not happen regularly. Some girls will experience periods that happen every six weeks for a couple of months and then every three weeks for the next couple of months. It can take a long time, often two to three years, before your periods fall into a regular cycle. By that time, you will notice that you have them around once every month.

Most girls experience periods that last around five days each month. However, some girls can have periods that are shorter or longer than that. Typically, a period can last between four and seven days. You might also notice that your period is heavier or lighter. Again, this varies between one girl and another and there is not a specific level of bleeding that is considered "normal." However, if you find that you have *very* heavy periods, you can always talk to your GP or another doctor to ask them about your worries or concerns.

When you first start your period, you will notice that you might feel uncomfortable and experience some pain and cramps. In the days leading up to your period, you can also get more spots than usual or feel very bloated. This is very common and you might even have other symptoms like feeling really sick or lightheaded when you get your period. If you have very bad cramps and pain during your period, try using a hot water bottle against your tummy and lying down for a while. You might also be able to take a painkiller if the cramps are very painful.

As well as experiencing pain, many girls and women notice changes to their mood before their periods start. As we have mentioned, the hormones that cause your period also affect the way that you feel. They can change your emotions and make you feel upset, annoyed and moody. You might feel like you want to be mean to the people around you such as your family and your friends.

Feeling like this can be scary because your body and your mind are not in your control at the moment. But this is normal and every girl goes through it.

One of the big decisions that you will have to make when you start your periods is whether you want to use a sanitary pad, a tampon or a menstrual cup. There are good and bad things about each of these which we will look at in more detail now.

○ **Sanitary Pads** – These are pads that sit inside the lining of your underwear. Often, they have a sticky strip to stick them to the material of your underwear so that they do not fall out. They come in a variety of shapes and sizes and you can get pads that are more suitable for lighter or heavier periods. They are often a good choice for younger girls because they are easy to use and you do not have to insert them inside your body. However, they can sometimes smell if you do not change them regularly enough.

○ **Tampons** – Some girls like to use tampons rather than pads. They can be really useful for when you go swimming or if you are playing sports because they can not slip inside your underwear in the same way that pads can do. Tampons work by being inserted into your vagina and they soak up the blood. However, if you decide to use tampons, you should change them very regularly. If you leave it inside your body for more than 6-8 hours, you can develop an infection called Toxic Shock Syndrome and this can be very serious.

○ **Menstrual Cups** – These are another option that you can use when you get your period and they work by inserting a cup into your vagina and allowing the blood to collect inside. When you remove it, you can empty it and rinse it out before using it again. Cups can be useful but they may be difficult to learn how to use when you are younger.

Periods are an important milestone in your life and they can often last until you are in your forties or fifties. Eventually, you will stop having your periods and go through something that is called the menopause.

Periods also show that your body has the ability to create human life. When you are older, you may have a baby and that baby will grow inside your body. Every time you have a period, this is your body's way of showing you how wonderful and magical your body really is and the amazing things that it is capable of.

BUYING YOUR FIRST BRA

The day that you buy your very first bra is a milestone in your life. It is a sign that you are growing up and starting to become a woman. It is important to remember that every girl develops at a different rate so do not be upset or worried if your friends are already wearing bras and you are not ready for one yet.

In the same way, if you are the first girl out of your friends to need a bra, that does not mean there is anything wrong with you. All it means is that you have just developed a little faster than them and they will start to catch up.

There is no specific age when you will need your first bra but you will notice signs that you are ready for one. It is always a good idea to visit a shop that offers a measuring service when you buy a bra, whether it is your first one or not. They will be able to fit you with the right size and style. There are many different types of bras – such as nonwired bras, crop tops, bralettes and sports bras - but do not buy underwired bras until you are much older as these can harm the tissue that is developing in your breasts. It is much better to wait until your breasts have grown fully before wearing an underwired bra.

When you choose your first bra, if your breasts are only just beginning to develop then a bralette or a crop top can be a good choice. They are a good way of getting used to wearing a bra before you need more support like you would get from a non-wired bra or a sports bra. Generally, non-wired bras can give you good support as you develop for your daily activities, like going to school or going to the shops. If you are very active and you play sports or during gym classes at school, wearing a sports bra is a good idea because it will give you a lot of support that you need.

There are also many different colours and patterns of bras to choose from. When you start out choosing your bra, it can be helpful just to pick a simple colour or pattern. Some bras have additions to them like lace but it's a good idea to keep in mind that these additions can be itchy or uncomfortable when you are not used to wearing them. You should also check your school's dress code too when you buy a bra. For example, if your school uniform is a white shirt, then wearing a black bra underneath might be against the school rules as it could show through the fabric.

It can be natural to feel self-conscious at first when you are wearing your bra but a good bra that is right for you should feel comfortable and give you the support that you need. It will also stop your nipples from showing underneath your clothes. It can stop you from getting aching breasts or feeling conscious that people are looking at you. For this reason, always try to go for a bra that is practical instead of one that looks fancy. Of course, you can find bras that do both but if you have to choose between a practical bra and a pretty bra, it is always better to go for the practical one.

When you feel that you are ready for a bra, try to talk to someone in your family, like your mum, and tell them that you want to start wearing a bra. If you talk to a woman, they will probably remember when they went to buy their first bra. It's also important to remember that if you do go bra shopping with your mum, it will probably be an emotional time for her too. To her, it will seem like yesterday that you were just a baby and now you are growing up and, on the road to becoming a woman. So, try and have a little patience with her if she says something that embarrasses you because all mums do this!

UNDERSTANDING FASHION

When you're young your parents pick out your clothes and help you get dressed. Then you get a little bit older and you can dress yourself. And now you're probably ready to start picking out your own clothes. How can we help you enjoy this exciting transition in your life?

The first thing to say is that your clothes show the rest of the world who you are. You're special and unique in your own way, so if you want to dress in a different way to other girls you know, that's great, well done you! And if you want to follow a trend because you love it, that's great too!

There's no right or wrong when it comes to your own fashion choices, they're just ways for you to express yourself. Sometimes you'll see a look you want to emulate online. Other times you'll come up with something all of your own creation. Plus there's always going to be times when you don't care about how you look because you just want to be comfortable. All of these are fine, they're natural, and adults feel exactly like this too.

Telling your parents that you like/don't like a particular style is a great way to get started. They'll help you have a bit more freedom when it comes to picking out clothes in the store. Then the rest is over to you and your own imagination. Enjoy it and you'll find that your self-esteem continues to grow and grow as you start growing up and begin to show the world who you are on the inside.

FOLLOWING CELEBRITIES

In today's world, celebrities are everywhere. From television actors to movie stars to the new, rising social media stars, it is difficult to escape celebrities and their lifestyles. If you use social media, read magazines or even watch television or movies, you will see these celebrities around a lot.

As a young girl, you might feel that you wish you had their wonderful lifestyle. It is natural to want to look good and have lots of money but many girls of your age can be harmed by trying to reach a beauty standard that is not possible without digital filters. Many celebrities do not look as good in real life as they do when you see them on television or in photographs. Remember that most of them have expensive makeup artists who work on them before they appear on television and they use filters and other effects on their pictures. They are not real women...

How important should celebrities be in your life?

Finding someone you look up to for what they've achieved is great. It could be a champion like Serena Williams, or it could be a leader like Michelle Obama. These are women who are celebrated for what they've achieved, not what they look like.

On social media there are thousands of influencers adding filters to airbrush the way they look. What you need to remember is that you're already perfect just the way you are, and you never need to try and live up to these unrealistic standards.

You're growing, learning, and having fun — your beautiful on the inside and on the outside. The most important thing at your age is to find things that make you happy and then spend as much time as you can doing them.

This is the part of your life where you can learn new skills, make new friends, and try new things. Do these three things and you'll find the beauty that lies inside you grows and grows, and with it so does your self-esteem.

Following celebrities can be fun sometimes, but the real women are the ones we celebrate for their achievements.

BENEFITS AND DANGERS OF THE INTERNET

The internet is an all-access pass to the entire world. You can find anything that you need online – from shoes to music to platforms that let you chat with your friends. There are many great things about the internet and it can be extremely useful.

When you have friends or family that you cannot see in person because they live far away, the web allows you to talk to them almost as if they were in the very same room as you. Also, when you are doing schoolwork for class, you can look up some helpful sites that can let you find the information you need to do a project or understand a subject for your homework.

The internet can even allow you to have your school classes online when it is not possible to go to school. For many children, this has been a way to keep them learning and stop them from falling behind.

But, while there are many good things about the internet, not everything about it is good. There are many downsides to the web and lots of dangers that you need to be careful of. There are dangers for both girls and boys but as a girl, there are some important things to watch out for, especially when it comes to predatory people and people making you feel bad about yourself and the way you look.

Internet grooming

There are some bad people who go online looking for younger girls that they can find and "groom" to do sexual things for them. These people can be men or women but they will often lie about their age or gender. For example, you might get a message from someone on social media who tells you that they are an 11-year-old girl. They might even have photos of a girl as their profile picture. But, when you cannot see them in person, it is difficult to know whether they really are who they say they are.

Of course, this doesn't mean you should refuse to reply to anyone who messages you but you will notice some warning signs if they are an adult who is trying to groom you to talk about or do sexual things with them.

For example:

O They may compliment your looks.

O They might write in a way that sounds "older" and be unfamiliar with the kind of slang that you use.

O They might try and turn the conversation into sexual things, such as asking if you have ever kissed a boy.

O They may ask you to send them pictures of yourself in underwear or even without any clothes on at all.

O They may want to see you on a camera but tell you that theirs is broken or that they do not have one.

○ They often will ask you not to tell your parents about your friendship with them and make you promise to keep it a secret.

○ Eventually, they might want to meet up with you and ask you to go to their house.

At first, it might seem like a confidence boost when someone is telling you that you look beautiful in your profile picture, especially if you have low self-esteem or body image issues. But, it can be a sign that all is not well with the person you are talking to and there is something "off" about them.

If you notice one or more of these signs with an online friend, then it is a good idea to talk to someone else and get another opinion. The best people to talk to are your parents but if this is not possible, talking to an older sibling, a family friend or even a teacher can help to keep you safe.

It is really important not to give in to the things that they want. So, for example, if you are talking to an online friend and they ask you to send a picture of yourself without clothes on, do not do it just because you want them to like you. Not only should they not be asking that, even if they are the same age as you are, but they could post your pictures online and lots of people could see them. Even when you get older, it is important to remember that.

Internet Addiction

It might sound strange but it is easy to become obsessed with spending time online. Many girls of your age spend a lot of time on the internet, browsing different websites and talking to their friends. But the internet can be harmful if you spend too much time online.

Spending hours online can stop you from going outside and having fun with your family and friends. It can also mean that you are sitting down for many hours and this can lead to weight gain and feeling tired a lot. You might notice that you become lazy when you spend too much time on the internet.

Bad Content

There are lots of things that you might stumble upon online that could be upsetting to you. Remember that nobody is guarding the web so anyone can post anything online. There are many young girls who see a picture or video that they wish they had not seen online.

If this happens to you, then it is important to talk to someone you trust and tell them what has happened. Talking about it can make you feel much better and you will not have to go through your upset, worry or sadness alone. Talk to a parent or friend if you find content that upsets you.

Cyber Bullying

Bullies have always existed. Even before the internet was a thing, many girls and boys were bullied at school or other places. Even adults can be bullied and it is nothing to be ashamed about if you have been or currently are a victim of bullying.

With the popularity of the internet, bullying has changed because bullies do not have to be in the same place as you to make you feel down or sad. Cyberbullying is becoming more common and if you experience it, you are not alone.

Many girls find they are the victims of cyberbullying.

Some of the signs of cyberbullying include:

O Receiving mean and nasty messages from people you know or strangers.

O Getting prank calls or messages.

O Having your social media account hacked.

O People spreading nasty and untrue rumours about you online.

You may feel jumpy, sad, nervous and even scared of leaving the house or going to school when you are being bullied as it can deeply affect your self-esteem. You might also feel angry and want to spend a lot of time alone but this can be unhelpful. It is really important to talk to an adult if you feel that you are being bullied as they can help to put a stop to it. Bullies are often cowards themselves. So, when you talk to an adult, you may find that they are not as brave as they have pretended to be.

If you experience any of these bad things when you are using the internet, the best thing to do is always to talk to someone. Of course, you might feel scared that your parents or guardians will be angry at you or judge you but they will likely almost always support you. However, if you really cannot talk to them, contact a children's helpline. The people who will answer your call are trained to deal with these kinds of things and they can give you some support and offer good advice that might make you feel better and find a solution.

FAMILY CONFLICTS

Conflicts at home can really harm your self-esteem and make you feel bad about yourself and your life. This can also impact the way you see yourself and your body, especially if you have a parent or a sibling who makes mean comments about you. Even if the fights are not connected with your body image, when you have lower self-esteem that can be bad for how you see yourself in general and can actually cause you to have a bad image of your looks.

Conflicts can happen with parents and/or your siblings. When you are growing up, you are constantly changing and developing. For most of your life, you have been a little girl but now you are heading toward your teenage years soon. For some of you, the teen years are still a little while away but for others of you, you are almost there.

During this time, you might feel that you want to have more independence and this can be one type of conflict that you find happens in your home. Conflict with your parents, especially as you are about to enter your teen years is common. Your mum and dad might not want to let go of that little baby, toddler and child that you have always been to them.

Of course, this does not feel good to you because you want to be able to learn more about the world. You feel curious and want to be able to have fun and go out with your friends to the shops or to the cinema or to get some food. It might be hard to understand now, but your parents will naturally be worried. They know that there are many dangers in the world and they want to protect you from them.

Talking to your parents can help. By expressing how you feel in a mature way, rather than shouting at them or sulking can show them that you are mature enough to be able to understand that you are growing up and how things are changing for you.

Another major type of conflict that can happen, and can be very upsetting for you, is when your mum and dad split up or get a divorce. Divorce means that a marriage is ending. But, keep in mind, if your mum and dad *do* split up, this does not mean that they do not love you anymore. They still love you just as much as they always did but they feel happier when they are not living together.

Of course, it can be very upsetting to hear your mum and dad arguing but you should also know that it is not your fault and you cannot change the way they feel about each other. Sometimes, two people still care about each other but they cannot live together anymore. The important thing is to understand that they still care about you.

In some cases, if you have grown up with a single parent or your parents are no longer together, meeting your mum's new boyfriend or your dad's new girlfriend can also make you feel confused. Suddenly, there is a new stranger in your life and they are becoming a part of your family. It can be easy to feel angry at them like they want to replace your parents or like they do not have a right to be in your life.

In this case, try and think about how much you love the parent who has a new partner. Do you want them to feel unhappy? Do you want them to feel lonely? When you love someone, like your mum or dad, you naturally want them to feel happy and the new person in their life is making them feel happy and stopping them from being lonely.

A new step-parent can cause conflict with your other parent too. Sometimes, they may feel hurt if you *do* like your new step-mum or step-dad. They might feel like you are on your other parent's "side". You are mature enough now to reassure them that you still love them even if you accept your new step-parent into your life too.

Dealing with difficult siblings – both older and younger – can be hard too. Many siblings find they fight about little things. If you have an older sister, for example, you might want to experiment and try on her clothes or use her makeup. This could make her feel angry and upset and can cause a fight between the two of you. It can be difficult to deal with and you might also feel angry and hurt that she doesn't want to share her things with you.

The four main types of sibling conflicts are:

O You with an older sister.

O You with a younger sister.

O You with an older brother.

You with a younger brother.

Different types of arguments can happen in all of these four situations. We will look at each type in more detail now.

The conflict between you and an older sister:

A time when fights can happen between you and an older sister is when you use your sister's favourite perfume that she got for her birthday. She smells the perfume on you and becomes very upset. She might call you names and grow angry and even tell your parents. This fight can be over very quickly or it can last for a long time.

How to resolve it?

Imagine that you are your sister and look at what's happening through her eyes. When you put yourself in her place, you will start to understand why she is upset. She sees her things as *hers* and she doesn't want to share them with you. That doesn't mean she doesn't care about you; it just means that she is also trying to figure out her identity and she has lots of thoughts and feelings, just like you do.

If you have taken something of hers without asking, apologise and explain that you have learned from what happened. Explain how you felt about her reaction and why it upset you, By talking to your older sister more openly, you can make your relationship with her a happier one. When you both get older, this can mean that you have a good friend as well as a sister in her.

The conflict between you and a younger sister:

Younger sisters can be really annoying at times, especially when they are always copying you and doing the same things you do. You might notice that your younger sister copies the kinds of clothes that you wear and listens to the music that you listen to. She might even want to hang out with you and your friends sometimes. It can make you feel irritated when your younger sister is trying to be like you and you might feel mad and resentful toward her like it's not fair that she wants to take everything that you like and make it her own.

How to resolve this conflict?

Firstly, it's important to understand that younger sisters often tend to look up to older sisters. You are like a role model to her. She wants to be like you because she probably thinks you are cool and funny and pretty. When she is your age, she wants to be just like you are now. This is a compliment.

Of course, that doesn't make it any less annoying when she is raiding your wardrobe or hanging out with you and your friends but trying to understand her can help you to feel more patient toward her.

The conflict between you and an older brother:

One of the most common types of conflict that might happen between you and an older brother is when he is too protective of you and it feels like he won't let you have any fun. In some ways, it could feel like he is trying to act like your dad, telling you where you can go and who with. He might tell you that you look silly when you try on makeup for the first time or if you wear new clothes that are very fashionable.

Over time, you might start to resent him because you don't like him telling you what to do and it's not fair that he has this power over you. Why should he get to tell you what you can and cannot do or wear? After all, he's not your dad!

How to resolve this conflict?

Older brothers naturally tend to want to protect their little sisters. It is called a natural instinct. Your brother might not realise how he is making you feel and why his behaviour is upsetting you. In fact, sometimes, even if you talk to him about it, he still might not understand why he is doing anything wrong. In his mind, he is keeping you safe from harm and stopping you from getting hurt.

Of course, there comes a point where it can be *too* much and you might need to talk to your parents if you feel that you are not getting the room to live your own life. As you approach your teenage years, you will want to have some more freedom than you have had during your childhood. Therefore, it is important to set some boundaries. Boundaries are the rules of what is and is not acceptable. So, for example, you can talk to your parents about setting boundaries for your brother's protectiveness. It might be acceptable for him to insist on going with you to a concert but it is not acceptable for him to scroll through your phone and read your messages from your friends.

The conflict between you and a younger brother:

Some girls think that their little brothers are the most annoying people in the world. He might make fun of you and want to be the centre of attention all the time. Sometimes, he might even try and embarrass you in front of your friends. Your parents might often blame you and tell you that you should be nicer to your brother, even when he's in the wrong.

How to resolve this conflict?

Young boys often try and get attention by being mean and annoying. They do not yet realise that girls do not like this. Your little brother is trying to get you to pay attention to him by doing these things that irritate you. So, when he jumps in a puddle and splashes you, in his mind, it is all just fun. Even if you yell at him, at least he is the centre of attention.

The best thing to do when your little brother does something that annoys you is to *ignore him*. What he really wants is attention. So, by giving him that attention, he is learning that doing something naughty gets him what he wants. However, when he is not annoying you, be extra nice to him. Then, he can learn that being nice makes people pay attention to him while being naughty means that he gets ignored.

Coping with a new baby in the house:

When a new baby comes along, your mum and dad might pay a lot of attention to them and not pay as much attention to you as they used to do. The baby might take up a lot of their time. It can be easy to become jealous and envious of your new baby sibling. You might dislike the way your parents spend so much time with them and less time with you.

As a girl at a stage of life when you are going through many different changes, it can be hard to understand why your parents are paying so much attention to the new baby. However, you should realise that this shows that they trust you and have faith in you. They know that you are not a *baby* anymore. Even though you still need their support and love, you are not helpless in the same way that a new baby is helpless.

How to resolve it?

If you feel that your parents have not been spending enough time with you, *tell them*. When a mum and a dad have a new baby in the house, that baby cries a lot and wants to be fed and changed all the time. So, it is easy for them to spend all their time doing those things without realising that they are not spending enough time with you.

Ask your parents to set aside some time each day or each week to spend with you. Talk to them about having family dinners together if you do not already do that. Most importantly, be clear with them how you are feeling and why you feel hurt by not having their attention like you used to do. They might not even have realised that you are feeling this way.

You should also try to keep in mind that having a new baby sibling does not mean that your parents love you any less than they did before. They just have a new life that depends on them too now. You might even find that it is fun to help out with looking after your new sibling, like at feeding or changing time. This will mean that you can make your parents less tired and give them more time to spend with you too.

Overall, resolving family conflicts and arguments that happen in the house can help to boost your self-esteem and make you feel better about yourself. This is even more true if you notice that your siblings or parents make mean comments about your appearance during arguments. Sometimes, people can "push your buttons." This means that they will purposely say something mean when they know that you already feel bad about that thing. Remember that does not mean they always mean what they say – they are just trying to get to you. But a more peaceful home life can make you feel better generally and give you extra confidence in other parts of your life.

MORE THAN "JUST A GIRL"

One of the most difficult things for girls of all ages to go through is discovering what it means to be a girl. There is a lot of focus on beauty and often, you might feel that this is all that matters. However, as you go through puberty and develop, you will also learn more and spend a lot of time in school. You will start to make decisions about what you are going to do with your life.

When society is so focused on the way you look, it can be hard to think about what you can do with your intelligence. However, looking at your other talents can be the perfect way to boost your self-esteem. Sometimes, as a girl, you will notice that there may be some barriers for you to overcome when it comes to people's attitudes.

Puberty can start as early as the age of eight, though for many girls it begins a little later. Almost all girls have started to show signs of puberty by the age of thirteen. As we have said, it can be easy to focus on the way you look without thinking about the other talents that you have. Looks are not everything in life and if you have other talents, it can help you to focus less on your looks and more on your other abilities.

When you turn eight, you will also notice other changes to your body and your mind as well as changes to the way that society sees you. As you get older, you will see differences in the way people treat boys and girls. When you were a little kid, nobody minded if you wanted to roll around in the mud with your brothers or your friends who are boys.

Now, people might start to want you to act like a little lady and behave in a certain way. However, at your age, you want something different. You finally understand more about the world and you want to talk about it and give your opinion. So, it can be frustrating if people do not want to listen to what you have to say. It can also harm your selfconfidence – the feeling that you have when you feel like you trust your own abilities.

From around 8 onwards, you might also start to develop an interest in things like the news and current events. You want to know more about what is going on in the world around you. Things that were boring before and "just for your parents" are now more interesting to you. As you learn more in school about things like climate change, politics and other topics, it is normal to want to talk about them.

But it is important to realise that girls are still breaking down some barriers in society. For many centuries, girls and women did not have the same kinds of rights that men had. While girls and women, especially in the west, now have equal rights to boys and men, some people still have an old attitude that girls should just act like ladies and not talk about current issues.

As a young girl, dealing with this issue can be really upsetting because you might feel confused as to why some people do not take you seriously or want to listen to you. Of course, most people are not like that. But if you do meet someone who does treat you in that way, remember that it is not your fault and they are the ones who need to change with society, not you.

You might also hear something called a "stereotype." A stereotype is when people have a fixed image of what a certain type of person should be. So, for example, some people still believe that only boys should be doctors and girls should become nurses. You might have heard that on the television or read it in books or magazines. You might even have heard other kids say it when you are in school.

When you hear these *stereotypes*, remember that they are not true. Being a girl does not limit you or prevent you from doing what you want to do. There are many women, now and throughout history, who have achieved incredible things.

Here are a few of them:

○ **Queen Elizabeth II of Great Britain:** The Queen is the longest-reigning monarch, either male or female, and has been on the British throne for decades. Not only is she the monarch of the United Kingdom but she also reigns over the Commonwealth too, which is a collection of countries that are independent but used to be under British rule. As well as being one of the world's most powerful women, the Queen has raised four children and has several grandchildren and great-grandchildren. She is an excellent example of a woman who has been able to "do it all."

O **Ruth Bader Ginsburg:** Although she passed away in 2020, Ruth Bader Ginsburg was a trendsetter for women who wanted to have careers and make their mark on the world. She was a judge on the United States Supreme Court and made very important decisions about the future of the USA in her job.

O **Emmeline Pankhurst:** One of the most famous Suffragettes – a group of women who fought for women to have the right to vote in political elections, Emmeline Pankhurst really helped women to gain equal rights. Although it was not easy for her, she made sure that your generation was able to do all the things that you like to do, just like boys your age are able to do.

○ **Rosa Parks:** As an African-American at a time in US history when black people did not have the same rights as white people, Rosa Parks stood up (or sat down) for what was right. By sitting down in the "white" section of a bus in Alabama, she helped to make the Civil Rights movement famous across the world. Her actions helped to make equality for all people a reality.

○ **Kamala Harris:** The first-ever female Vice President of the United States of America, Kamala Harris has helped to change attitudes about women and ethnic minorities. She had been very successful in her career and proved that times are changing for women and girls.

○ **Queen Elizabeth I of England:** Queen Elizabeth I was a woman who was born into a man's world. The second daughter of King Henry VIII, she was never viewed as a good option to become the ruler of England because she was a woman. However, she ended up being one of the greatest rulers in English history. She managed to stop the Spanish Armada from invading England and

○ **Marie Curie:** This female scientist was the firstever person to win two Nobel prizes – a prize that people get for great achievements in subjects like chemistry, physics and literature. Along with her husband, she discovered some chemical elements and made great strides for women in the scientific field.

○ **Ada Lovelace:** If you've ever heard anyone say that girls cannot do science or maths, Ada Lovelace was proving them wrong centuries ago. She was the daughter of the poet, Lord Byron and is thought of as the first female computer programmer, even though she was born in 1815, long before modern computers were invented.

○ **Malala Yousafzai:** The youngest ever person to get a Nobel prize, Malala went through a lot of hardship when she was a little girl. She was born in Pakistan and wanted girls to be able to go to school, just like boys. She fought very hard to help girls get the same rights as boys had.

As you grow up and get older, remember the achievements of all these women if people tell you that you are "just a girl" or if they say you cannot do something because you are only a girl. You are more than just a girl – you are strong and it is always important to remember that you can do all the things that boys can do. So, if you want to be a successful doctor, scientist or footballer, you can do those things. Other girls and women are doing them very well.

In life, you will likely meet some people who *do* believe that being a girl stops you from doing things. Those people are not important because more and more people know that times have changed and girls have a world of opportunity at their feet.

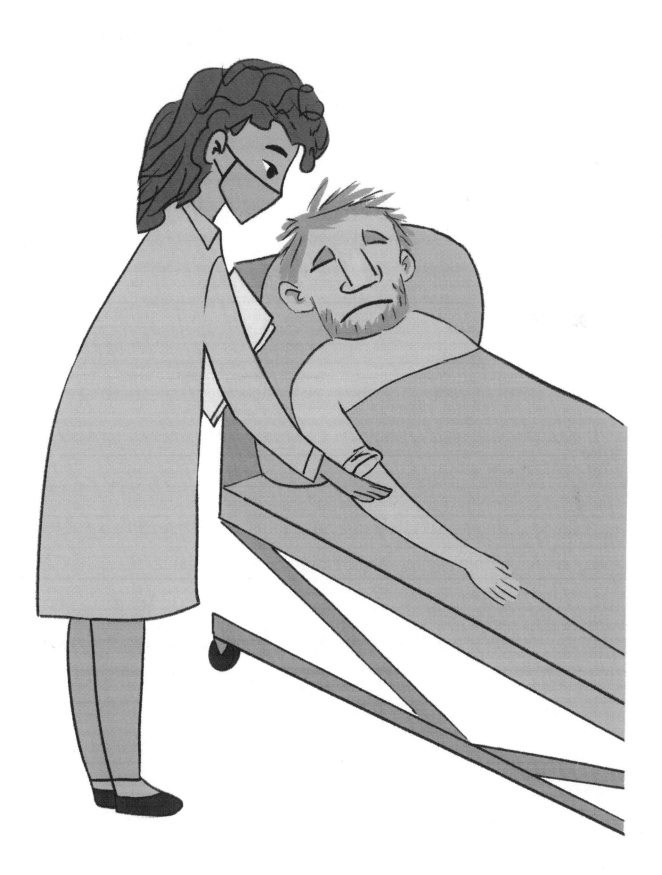

BOYS AND RELATIONSHIPS

As you head toward high school, or you may already be in high school, you are probably starting to see boys differently from the way you used to see them when you are younger. As you get older, you start to produce hormones as we discussed in the chapter about approaching puberty. These hormones are running wild inside your body, stirring up new feelings and emotions.

For the first time in your life, you might start to realise that boys are attractive. You might even develop your first crush on a boy in your class or a neighbour boy that you see around your local area. At first, this can be scary. Your face might feel hot and flushed, your heart might race in your chest and you may feel like you have butterflies fluttering in your tummy.

This is a big milestone in your life and it is important not to underestimate it. As you start to feel crushes on boys, you might also become more aware of how you look. You will probably feel like you want that cute boy to think you are also cute.

At this point, it can be easy to fall into the trap of changing the way you look to make a boy like you. Some girls change the way they dress, trying to look older and more mature. Other girls start wearing makeup because they think it will make them look better. However, a boy who is really worth taking the time to get to know will not be concerned with whether you wear makeup or whether you are wearing jeans and a jumper or a dress.

If a boy *really* likes you and respects you, then he will value what is on the inside as much, if not more than what is on the outside.

At the same time, it is important to know that not every boy will like every girl. Some boys have a type of girl that they like when it comes to looks. If you are not a specific boy's "type", that doesn't mean there is something wrong with you. There are other boys who will like the way you look.

When you first start to get interested in boys, it can be upsetting if a boy doesn't like you back. But, over time, you will realise that there are plenty of boys that like you – some of them you will like and others you will *not* like. This is just a part of life and a part of growing up for everyone.

BODY CARE AND SELF-ESTEEM

Taking care of your body is important for your health, but self-esteem always starts on the inside. Loving and accepting who you are is the best way to begin the process of caring for yourself and boosting your self-esteem.

Your body is the only body you will ever have:

It might sound strange to you but, of course, you will only ever have one body and that is the one that you have right now. Your body does a lot for you but you may feel like sometimes, you are not kind to it. You might look for small flaws and faults. Some girls are smaller and some girls are larger but all girls are beautiful in their own way. Therefore, it is important to look at the ways that *you* are beautiful and how you can feel good about the qualities that you have.

Take a look at yourself in the mirror and, instead of seeing any flaws, look at all the good qualities that you see. Start with your face and work your way to your body. For example, do you have bright skin? Do you have big, beautiful eyes? Do you have nice teeth and a nice smile? Do you have a cute nose?

Now, turn your attention to your body. Focus on yourself and see the good points. Are you tall or more petite? Keep in mind that both taller girls and more petite girls have good qualities. Are you thin or chubby? Again, remember that you are beautiful no matter what size you are. In some cultures, being skinny is considered to be ideal but in other cultures being a bigger girl is considered perfect. Beauty standards are not just set by the culture in the country where you live. Different people consider different shapes and sizes to be pretty.

However, sometimes you might want to make changes to the way you look. For example, if you feel that your hair is not stylish enough and is not similar to the current trends that you see your friends wearing or you see on celebrities, then it is normal to want to be fashionable. In this case, talk to your parents about getting a haircut and explain to them that you want to be in fashion like other people.

At the same time, remember that you are an individual. Some girls prefer to follow their own style and this is great too. If you have a specific type of fashion that you like, even if some people might consider it "old fashioned" then you should stick to what you like. This shows that you are your own person and that you have your own mind, which will be very important as you progress into the next stage of your life and when you finally reach your teenage years.

Learning to praise yourself:

It is very important to understand how essential praising yourself can be when it comes to boosting your self-esteem. If there are times when you feel down or like you are not good enough, this is the perfect time to tell yourself how good you are.

At first, it might feel really weird to tell yourself these sentences of praise. You might even feel like you do not believe them when you hear yourself say them at first. Of course, the point of this is to say them over and over at regular times until you start to believe them.

Here are some practical sentences that you can say to yourself to help you feel better when you are feeling down, sad, upset or stressed out:

- I am worthy of being loved and having good friends

- I am beautiful and my body is beautiful

- I am smart and good at schoolwork

- Good people like me and mean people do not matter

- My family cares about me and they will always support me

- Bad times always pass and better times will come

You can even write these sentences down on pieces of paper and stick them up in your bedroom so that you can see them to remind yourself of them often. Whatever it is that is affecting your self-esteem, you can use these phrases to boost your confidence and remind yourself of the skills and abilities that you have.

In fact, making a list of all of your best qualities is an excellent way to raise your confidence too. You can use this table below to make that list and write down all the good things about yourself.

My good quality	Examples of it	Why I should appreciate it

Below, you will also find an example of the table so that you can use it to help you fill in your own personal table:

My good quality	Examples of it	Why I should appreciate it
I am smart	I get good marks on my schoolwork	I can use this skill when I grow up to get a good job and make a lot of money
I have a nice smile	My friend complimented me on my smile	A nice smile shows that I am a friendly person and other people like to be around friendly people

I am generous	I gave my little brother some money from my allowance to buy a comic book that he really wanted	Being generous shows that I have a good heart and that I'm kind. Not everyone has that quality

CONCLUSION

As you have worked your way through this book, you will have learned a lot about the different things that are going on in your body right now or will start to happen in the very near future. You will now also be more familiar with how to appreciate your body and what it means to love yourself and increase your levels of self-esteem.

If you are confused about the changes in your body, do not worry because this is normal. Most young girls feel a little strange about these new changes that are taking place. As time goes on, they will come to feel natural and you will notice that you adjust to all the new feelings that are happening right now.

Over time, you will grow into your new body as long as you allow yourself the chance to love it. Do not forget to keep praising yourself. Even if you are feeling good about yourself for a while and you think that you do not need to boost your own confidence, you can always take the time and space to allow yourself that increase in self-esteem.

Over the next few years, as you become a teenager and beyond, you will face many challenges when it comes to body image. With the media full of what it means to be "perfect", it is easy to be influenced.

At those times, it is important to think about the main thing – you are already perfect the way you are. Even when you change and grow, everything that makes you *who you are* is lovable and there are a lot of people in the world that will be able to see that and appreciate you.

Your journey from girlhood to a teenager to becoming a woman is an exciting one that will give you some surprises and a lot of joy. Time often goes by very quickly so it is important to enjoy it because, one day, you might look back and realise it was one of the most exciting times in your whole life.

DISCLAIMER

This book contains opinions and ideas of the author and is meant to teach the reader informative and helpful knowledge while due care should be taken by the user in the application of the information provided. The instructions and strategies are possibly not right for every reader and there is no guarantee that they work for everyone. Using this book and implementing the information/recipes therein contained is explicitly your own responsibility and risk. This work with all its contents, does not guarantee correctness, completion, quality or correctness of the provided information. Misinformation or misprints cannot be completely eliminated.

Made in the USA
Las Vegas, NV
10 December 2024